WONDERLAND

New and Selected Poems

Sarwat Zahra

Translated from the Urdu by Rizwan Ali
and Robert Schultz

Also by Sarwat Zahra

poetry collections in Urdu

Song of the Blazing Wind

From Time's Prison

WONDERLAND

New and Selected Poems

Sarwat Zahra

ACKNOWLEDGMENTS

The author would like to thank the editors of *The Hudson Review* who first published the English translations of "A Scene of Sorrow While Traveling," "The Queen of the Internet," and "A Butterfly Without Wings" in Volume LXXII, Number 4 (Winter 2020).

Cover painting by Shaista Momin
Cover design by Arshad Ali
Author photo by Mussarat Abbas

WONDERLAND: New and Selected Poems

ISBN 9781667816708

For Rizwan Ali

WONDERLAND

CONTENTS

Song of the Blazing Wind (2009)

New Poems

Ghazal, *Only I existed and you*

Before this Earth, before even Time, only I existed and you.
Before sight or even imagination, only I existed and you.

Before thoughts climbed stairs and dreams rubbed their eyes,
Before morning's call, only I existed and you.

Before light brightened and the world grew full,
Before things seen and things unseen, only I existed and you.

We stand onstage in outlandish costumes;
Before we debased ourselves like this, only I existed and you.

The body counsels restraint, but I talk back;
Before being arose in any way, only I existed and you.

Our simpleton god knows nothing of love, nothing of passion.
Even before my marrow quickened, only I existed and you.

Ghazal, *Restless beauty*

Every dream fell asleep, but thought stayed awake.
We swallowed answers, but questions would not sleep.

Dreams weighed on our eyes, so not for one night,
For a week or a season, then not for years did we sleep.

All that time without you! Strange wounds pressed deep.
When I finally saw you regret would not sleep.

Once, at last, my memory touched your presence,
And afterwards that beauty would not sleep.

Beauty tossed us so many nights
Our listless bodies—leaden—would not sleep.

What caused all this? We never thought to ask.
All our lives, not asking why, we do not sleep.

Gilgamesh Searches Still

Great God has tied the rainbow of Time
To the ends of the sky
And lullabies me in the tongues of desire.
Yet I do not sleep—
  I do not sleep!
  Duhai! Duhai!

Earth provides a sandlewood seat,
A solid dream for vanishing life
Through all of time.
On command the galaxies stop for me!
But I do not sleep—
  I do not sleep!
  Duhai! Duhai!

Fresh henna swirls on eternity's hands,
Its forehead is flushed with desire.
But I do not sleep—
  I do not sleep!
  Duhai! Duhai!

As I tip and balance, the seven skies
Open a space where I set my pieces—
My ivory pieces—to start a new game,
Yet I do not sleep—

I do not sleep!
Duhai! Duhai!

When desire's seedling finds my body,
Its richest loam, the Earth goes giddy,
Loaded with green,
And I do not sleep—
I do not sleep!
Duhai! Duhai!

Heer's Coat Hook

In Waris Shah's epic of Heer, Prince Ranjha escapes
trouble at home by disguising himself as a beggar
and departing to a rival town, where the king hires
him to be a cowherd. There he falls in love with
Princess Heer, and she with him, whereupon her
family forces her into an arranged marriage with a
prince she does not love. This poem is said by Heer,
who is addressing a coat hook which, magically,
has spoken to her.

Why must you ask me to bare my heart,
To hang up its clothes *now*?
Time itself stands naked,
      perplexed.

The land of dreams has nine doors,
And behind each one a hundred promises.
But inside and out, my being remains
      a desert.

From the green clay of its unfired pots
      the stench of thirst cries out.
Even in stream beds the land crumbles.

Please, someone, call my name!
Ranjha is lost—a wandering beggar.
>*Fill his bowl with alms!*

When desire rushes from my heart's door
With its tray of goods
My body recovers its nakedness
And my soul its respect.

Break-up in Spring and Diwali

You set fire to our dream,
Dropped it on my heart's doorstep,
And left to find your Paradise.

I'm still wrangling with God
To stay out of hell, so how do I
Put this *new* fire out?

Like a string of fireworks tossed
By children, threads pop,
My fabric tears.

And my tender kite-strings
Keep unspooling
As Time's sharp line threatens.

You knew what you were doing.
You mapped in advance
Where to plant your mines.

Now, unready, I walk
This field, unable to stand
Spring's fragrance.

Facebook's New Friend

Facebook has a new friend. Death,
From its eternal home, enters,
Silent, the Timeline.

Numbers, infinite, spin.
Emojis, frozen, convey no emotion.
Pictures flicker on coals.
Every status is ashen.

Knitted words unravel now. Letters fall.
Lines step to a mourner's tambourine.

Profile pictures hold their breaths.
Every photo in every album—
All that churning in emotion's ponds—
Dries into dust. All eyes and hearts
Fill with dust.

Nervous dreams spread in waves
Beyond the internet's limits.
Cultch jams poetry's throat.
When death's enormous gong sounds
The web stills.

Facebook has a new friend, Death.

Sheol

Between Heaven and Earth,
In this place—this *Sheol*—
I play at living.

Between positive and negative
I turn every day to my "window time"
To peer at life.

Between day and night
I walk this road—this twilight road—
Where breath trades away its air.

Between right and wrong
Stands a question mark.
On its hook hangs my entire being.

Between white and black,
Through this gray zone's tiny window,
I measure all things—the world's whole breadth—

An unending job. Always here, in this in-between,
Sheol digs certainty's grave
Within me.

From Time's Prison

Wonderland

Before the collar was the neck,
And before the neck, one upon one,
The vertebrae's nested ascent.

Before pen and ink, the finger,
And before the finger, its reaching nerves.
Before sounds, the mouth, this tongue enlivened
By an intricate tatting.

When invisible stays pulled the tent of the eye's
Full whiteness round, the pupil opened
And spectacle followed. But even before
The eye took shape: eons of travel,
Time's dark abyss.

Behold this Journey!
And before the first steps
An intention moved—
You in my heart, primordial longing
Issuing first from the stench of caves,
My helix scratched on their walls—

And before the before
And before once more,
What first divide?

A Scene of Sorrow While Traveling

In the disgusting market, flushed youth—
These blossoming faces!—
It's all for sale.

Earth stretched out beside its river
Is dying for a drink.

Life, itself! Vendors sell its labor pangs
For a handsome price.

The New World Order! Its rising flames
Singe the fortune tellers' charts.

My fellow travelers carry on their backs
This blood-stained road.

At the great crossroads, reporters cry out
Yesterday's news, lending voice to terror.

The man on the dump surveys his domain:
Under tin and rubble, upturned hands
Clasp cigarette butts, torn collars;
The beggar-woman's grubby coins
Sit in her bowl, her cries silenced.

Oil bubbles in a blackened vat.
The future fries.

Sewer waters flush every
Youthful, dream-filled eye.

On a street corner, when a free man whistles
The notes burn to ash.

In the market today, every stock tip
Is bullish on sorrow.

Mirror, Mirror

Mirror, Mirror, on the wall,
Speak of our time . . .

The Organization for the Peoples' Welfare
Forges sickles for flowers;

The Food Program ships cough syrup—
The narcotic kind—in baby bottles;

The Statistics Bureau makes its census report
Counting condoms in sewers;

For the popcorn harvest, the Ag Council
Sends farmers manure laced with salt;

The Organization for World Peace
Has decided to sponsor the WWF;

And those who swallow the daily news grow obese . . .

The mirror speaks of what is to come—O these days!—
Then shatters and falls.

What Birds Want

On the cold railings of high-rise apartments
Surviving birds don't ask for much—
A little silence, a little freedom.

Where smoke hangs heavy, their morning flights
Seek a clear sky, and freedom.

In the flight paths of lumbering jets,
Scattering birds seek only space
And a little freedom.

Where plastic bags clog sewer grates
Birds sip the trickling water. They long for rain,
For a long drink and some freedom.

Birds only want that bright feeling
Of first flight, of a world alive
In shining blue skies,
That freedom.

The Meal of Being

On this bright cloth spread before me,
In bowls made of pain, I am served endurance.
This we must eat.

I chew dream candies
And bite my tongue.
We must taste this blood and sugar.

My skin's stuffed with touch
Like a pepper. Savor it!
And save it—please!

Pain sours like milk—makes kafir
So white its light spreads from courtyard to sky.
Hide this light in your eyes!

Fear bursts its jars!
It poisons my thoughts. But remember
This feast of pictures—please!

A Butterfly Without Wings

With dust I fall from the duster.
I spin in the whirr of the ceiling fan.
I dance in the curry's rising scent.

I am rolled between the pin and its board.
I'm bread on the griddle. I scorch on it.
I'm the pot's high whistle—its cry!
And now, in the pan, I lie and simmer—
      Still alive!

Working Mother

Mom-eeey!

Do you *have* to go to the office?

Mussst you go? How will I sleep?

When will you come back?

Mom-eeey! The maid smells funny.

How will I eat?

Will you call me? *Call me!*

Sunday will you stay home, at least?

At the doorstep daily, teary cheeks,

Burning questions on tiny lips,

My little girl's eyes frozen wide.

She nearly trips me—city so far—from my feet.

The Female Gaze

Deen Zamana Khan!
Your generations are born of women,
These "filthy" creatures
Who must never walk in daylight.

Deen Zamana Khan!
A woman's breath kindles your woodstove,
But, dizzy with joy, this butterfly
Must not dance on a breeze.

Deen Zamana Khan!
Your bed is watered by the rain of fruitful women,
But their love cries and lovely dreams
You bury in layers of sleep.

Deen Zamana Khan!
Your courtyards bloom with needlework flowers
While women's screams
Die in the graves of their bodies.

Deen Zamana Khan!
You celebrate the harvest's bounty,
Guzzling the milk of paradise, ruling as god,
But the pure high note the women hold
Will not last long.

Deen Zamana Khan!
Your tall white turban is starched by women
Who tie your shoes, who braid your waistbands,
While the sheets they wear, black in every season,
Remain mired in night.

From Futility's Cross

On futility's cross, I hang. Spikes pierce,
Blood flows, and the throng cries poison.
Truth, like a mountain, bears down on us all,
Yet the crowd clamors for more.

Curses, whistles, even silence wounds.
Hypocrisy's cheap! You can buy it in any shop!
When spikes pierce and blood flows
Stay quiet to survive, stay calm to persist.

Lies and fear are strangers to me.
I've committed no crimes, I don't riot,
Yet malice flies—volleys of arrows—
And spikes pierce, blood flows.

The Sky Has Swallowed Them

With every sound I think he's back—
There's not enough food in the pot!—
But he's not.

He's been gone so long . . .
The sun goes up, the sun goes down—
In the courtyard his shadow
Looms and hides.

Who is that in the mirror?
Who appears in my eyes like votive candles
Flickering?

What mystery glints
While I stucco fresh mud over silence?
In your long absence
My body and soul have gone cold.

From the front door to our bedsheet's corner,
My hope, your image, wavers.
The children help me hold it.

Time Needs Sleep

When dew drenches the arches
Of churches, the synagogues' stairs,
The domes of mosques, a threadbare blanket
Covers the beggar who sleeps in the street.

Desires cast upon water all night
Have turned the oceans to oil.

Hands that fed the park's fishes
Have returned to their jobs.

Naked feet that whispered together
While couples on beaches counted waves
Now will only meet in their beds.

Seagulls' wings that quilled clear breezes
Now must learn to write with smoke.

The tottering morning,
Arm-in-arm with the time-worn sun,
Staggers, groggy, away.

Time Does Not Heal All Wounds

This game, Snakes and Ladders, disgusts me.
The numbers engraved on my heart's dice
Cramp my style.

I always lose. The cobra of my silky dreams
Sees through my ruse and swallows my every move.

The ladder I climb collapses.
Its rungs—brittle bones—break off when I step.

When I make my move to a green square
It becomes my grave. I can't breathe!

Time—my opponent—our game must end.
Let us agree: beginning today you are free.
And me.

Life Is Not a Logarithmic Problem

I want to dance only with you!
But angles, triangles, circles, and squares
Make a fool of me.

Life is not a logarithmic problem
One pays to have solved. When I think like this
A corner breaks free from its square,

A star jumps from the night sky,
A boat tilts on a fresh breeze
And laughs at its silly mistake.

The star traces a line in the mirror,
Returns to itself, and my frozen figures
Warm themselves in its light and dance.

My feet step free of your love triangle,
But my dream trips on its silken threads
That wrap me up, cocooned.

Help me escape!
Again, by the campfire,
I want to dance only with you!

$E=mc^2$

O Earth! I want to be freed from these narrow halls!
You should not be snared in this net of orbs.
I should not be fixed by your compass points,
By centers and tangents. But O!—my nerves!
My umbilical cord!—it trembles, attached
By gravity's tug to the spinning planets.
My filthy body is dirt and rock like them.

But my blood knows, my Mercurial blood
Speeds its message, the same old message
From the light of my eyes to my heart.
And my heart carves every moment,
My fond old heart in its Venus trap,
A slave digging an endless trench,
Its yearly orbit.

Icy Saturn wants to rule my lands,
Wants to swallow my weekends.
But a stronger god—my mind robed
In the Seven Heavens—binds me to Mars,
That fiery god with his questions and weapons.
He readies for war to free the goddess, my Venus.

O, but the Oceans—those gods and their storms!—

Their cyclones take me—

Free me, Venus, from these narrow halls!

The Queen of the Internet

On your throne of clouds, O Queen of Dreams,
How long will your silken fingertips
Stitch hope on our palms?

Beauty rises in your brilliant courtyard—
Flashing pictures, dreamy illusions, red velvet mites,
Full ripe grapes to make us drunk.
Yet even here, from a cistern brimming
With loneliness, a drop splashes out.

In a crowded café you flash bright signs:
Love and desire—burning lips, laughter and sobs.
But everything here is just half-true, a moment's façade.
You'll drown in your clouds,
O Queen of Dreams!

In crowded chat rooms, icy hearts
Devour emotions, gnaw raw souls,
Choking behind their human masks.
Loneliness does its colorful dance on burning words.
How long will you fan their dying embers?

O Queen of Dreams on your throne of clouds,
Thirst will finally ask for rain.

Song of the Blazing Wind

Ghazal, *My glass dress*

Light has eaten my glass dress
And the day's joy devours the night.

Love's madness is my last devotion.
Submission has consumed the rest.

The body staggers—every sinew sags—
But thirst gulps down the soul's brightness.

When bitterness blunts my every desire
Knowledge has swallowed innocence.

Words learned sunlight's language
So feelings can feed these poems.

Ghazal, *I make thousands of homes*

I make thousands of homes that wait for you—
So many doors—new passage-ways!

All day the quotidian shreds my dreams.
At night I stitch my bed from the moments.

In our time the dancers have no feet.
I write bodies, unfinished, their heads bowed down.

I discover the heights of deprivation.
I make oceans and beaches signify thirst.

Imagination, fueled by feelings, knows no bounds.
I remake the earth, spread a limitless sky.

But these feelings die entombed in words.
Who can know what I've made within!

Disposable

Am I a tissue that sits in a pocket
Awaiting your need
When a wound starts to ooze?

Or am I a bottle of fine cologne
Passing long hours on the dressing table,
Attending your hour of desire?

Or am I one of your razor blades—
That special brand—to be kept
From rust, used, and thrown out.

Or am I that checkbook—
Those secret checks in that secret account
Locked in your briefcase, honored to ride
      near those memorable photos?

Or am I simply a can of soda—
Sealed and pure, to be opened here
Or elsewhere later—to slake your thirst
      and be tossed?

Don't Be Scared

Don't be scared.
I'll take care
Of my womb.

I have cleansed it with fear—
Disgrace, family, the gaze of others—
A perfect hygiene, like DDT.

Don't be scared.
I've chained her down,
Every crack sewn shut.

If my soul tunnels,
I'll shovel cold dirt
To block its escape.
Every month I'll strangle
Its cries.

If my dreams bear arms
And mass at your border,
Preparing invasions,
We'll slay them.

Eve's Daughter

I am Eve's daughter, that's my crime.
And now—a poem!—the *greatest* crime.

Why should I have feelings?
I just meet a need.
(This thought itself is a crime.)
And now—a poem!—the *greatest* crime.

I am *not* a spectacle. I speak my mind.
I think, so I should be hanged?
When I open my mouth it's a crime.
And now—a poem!—the *greatest* crime.

Even with my hem on fire I clench my teeth.
Bearing injustice, I *must* stay quiet.
When I open my mouth it's a crime.
And now—a poem!—the *greatest* crime.

I jail my feelings—my heart's a prison.
How dare I insult you!
Even to utter your name is a crime.
And now—a poem!—the *greatest* crime.

Free Will Is Not So Free

I stole little gods from the Light,
And now in my chest they dance like fire.

From Time I took water to quench my thirst—
And now it blisters my soul.

I stole touch from Evening
And feel myself so strange a being
I can find no way
To ferry my days into night.

Who shares my illness
Sleeps not. Not for a moment
Thought from madness finds refuge.

Galileo Must Not Recant

Raif Badawi—
Galileo must not recant.

Truth again must untie the knots
At Mansoor's neck.

Socrates must baptize himself
Again in hemlock's dreams.

Prometheus must grow his liver again
To feed new eagles.

To keep time turning, Mukhdoom Bilawal, oil its gears!
Render your body to the grindstones again!

Raif Badawi,
Bruno's trial is reconvened. His body burns.
Extinguish the flames with your fresh blood.

The great clock chimes Two Thousand Fifteen
And Mary's son must hang from its dials.

Hussain again, his head piked on his own spear,
Must trudge the streets, parting hushed throngs.

Raif Badawi—

Again Galileo must not recant.

Heritage

Life was bequeathed a love of mirrors
And mirrors hold her Love's reflection.

Life will ever gaze at reflections,
Will ever kiss Love's frozen shapes.

Smash the mirrors to touch Love's warmth!
But Life was bequeathed a love of mirrors.

Housewife

I have become a bottle of milk
For my kids,
Satisfaction for Master,

A machine that cleans.
And for myself?
The softest whisper of movement.

In my house, where I sleep,
Solitude-swaddled both night and day,
I'm hot to the touch.

I pretty myself with woven bracelets
That stink with my thoughts.
I redden my lips with questions.

Loneliness answers departing kisses.
My pupils dilate, black without kohl
To search deep silence.

I smile through tears.
I'm a thing in the house,
The housewife.

Hut

This cottage stands on powdery sand.
Beached for a while, you've made it your motel.
This house, this hut, is a comfortable stop
For a few coins, for a little while.

Weathered, it suffers the seashores thunderous winds.
Plaster falls from its walls and ceiling.
The porch shades have lowered their gaze in shame,
But the winds still roar.

Each new arrival has scarred these hallways,
Carving his name in a heart. Each pretends
This house is home, though its walls are filled—
So many pierced hearts!

Nibbled crusts and leaning towers of dirty dishes
Litter the kitchen, but its stove has never been lit.
Nothing here finds its proper place:
Bedroom, living room—every space

Is thoroughfare to your dripping feet.
Doors wary of sudden blows
Fear to close completely.
It feels as though the hut grows restless.

It wants to flee the ocean's horrible roar,

But stranded here between ocean and city,

It crumbles to sand.

In Search of

My umbilical cord was cut at birth.
I absorbed half, and half was buried in earth.
Since then I have searched for my lost half.

At first I searched my mother's womb
And my father's eyes, but despite my digging
I could not find it.

Then I plumbed my lover.
Perhaps by mistake it was buried in him.
For years I searched. I dug and delved,
And found at last in my lover's soul a lost piece.
But it proved to be his, hidden deep.

Then I thought my cord had become the body of my child.
But as he's grown he's begun to search for his own.

So I've given up, though now I'm sure
My cord, like a worm, will find me in my grave.

Museum

Before my eyes, my life has become a museum.
Without my knowing, my unconscious amassed
Its secret treasures, its antique blessings.

Mummified words and lacquered moments,
Stacked on shelves, stand protected
Even from the heat of my body!

Broken bangles sound from drawers,
Little tambourines. Look at this shelf—
See the broken body of my childhood doll.

On my dressing table its cracked mirror
Holds hellish moments. Did I lose my eye?
It stares back at me from the kohl pot!

My life wails, crushed beneath its rusted jewelry,
Spooked by the clink of my bangles.
A broken comb holds tangled hairs.

Off in a corner a pitcher leaks the scent of my thirst.
The stuck dial of a great clock trembles upon
        a painful moment.
From swamps of emotion a stench wafts up.

Hoards of tourists arrive to ogle my house of wonders.

One exclaims, "It's nothing but a gasping corpse!"

Another, a scholar, sifts my leavings, but only

      to show off his genius.

None will discover the vital thread hidden in dust.

I stand aside, waiting at the end to be found.

New Millennium

Fish bang their heads in a bowl.
We shiver in rooms of glass.

As if birds fear wind,
Recorded twitters issues from speakers.

We pass whole seasons, our air conditioned.
Artificial showers water our flowers.

Life is washed in Surf and Tide,
And Lite is sold in bottles.

Between soul and body, fog drifts.
Where shall we look to find our shadows?

Smoke rises from Earth to space,
Blackens night's eyes without kohl.

Dust coats our glasses, lights glare,
So how can we see—tell me

How can we see
His face?

Pregnant Winds

Far away two letters joined and made a sound,
Then roaming winds swept it up.

But why do these winds shy away from birds,
From even the gentle butterfly's wings?

How softly they step, how they seem to brood
On their billowing shapes, on their changed condition.

Now I see! It is spring
And these winds are pregnant!

.

Now their wailing assaults my ears.
They bang at my door.

They cry for me, but I stay quiet,
And all the town's Christians stay silent, too.

We worry, we're scared—
The whole city fears

These pregnant winds,

This pregnant world.

What might we lose?

But what might we gain?

Song of a Blazing Wind

Again wind pierces my clothes,
Comes near to my body—from pore to pore
Evening swings in delight.

Again wind burns for a dream,
Sweeps to my eyes and fills my pupils,
Blurs every shadow with ashes.

Wind parches my lips, tips
My glass, splashes the wine,
And the wind, then, swallows fire,

Scorches my body, torches
My soul—fire! fire!
And the wind—

The Interrogation

What is your name?

Life!

In this city of silence life is a crime.
You are charged with the crime of living.

What do you do?

I pray!

To pray is a crime in the marketplace.
In every street, in every bazaar,
In this whole precinct prayer is a crime.
You are charged with the crime of praying.

Where do you live?

This is my road!

This is my street!

Look at yourself! Your pestilent dreams!
Their germs cling to your body!
You'll infect the city! You are charged
With spreading unsanitized dreams.

What are you hiding
Beneath your eyelids?

Sir, only light!

So you dare to steal light! Thief!

You are charged with stealing daylight.

We've got you this time!

Poet Sarwat Zahra

Sarwat Zahra (b. 1972) has been recognized with 20 poetry prizes and citations by organizations in her native Pakistan, in the United Arab Emirates, and in India. Most recently, in October 2019, *Bazm-e Sadaf*, the Urdu poetry organization with chapters in ten countries, honored her with its prestigious international literature award. She writes in free verse and in the traditional ghazal form, addressing contemporary realities—popular culture, the internet, science, work, and the daily news—in a variety of forms and dictions. She writes frankly about women's issues, ranging from matters of romance to social justice. She addresses current political events, the "male gaze," and the situation of working mothers in poems of lament or protest, yet she also writes of romantic love, often contributing to the tradition of love poems that shade into metaphysical thought and religious yearning.

Her first book, *Song of the Blazing Wind* (2003), was issued in a second printing in 2009. Her second book, *From Time's Prison* (2013) was translated from the Urdu into Hindi in 2017. She has read her work widely as a featured poet at events in South Asia and the U.S., including recent major Urdu poetry gatherings in New York City and Washington, DC. Four of her poems, translated for the first time into English, appeared in *The Hudson Review* (Winter 2020) in versions prepared by Rizwan Ali and Robert Schultz and authorized by the poet. Dr. Zahra is a medical doctor specializing in emergency care. She lives and works in Dubai.

The Translators

Rizwan Ali, a published poet in his native Urdu, has been an invited participant and featured poet at conferences in New York City and Washington, DC. Ali has been a pioneer in the use of the internet to publish, share, and discuss Urdu literature. He founded the "Literary Forum of North America" on the literature of South East Asia which includes 2,500 members from 46 countries. He founded and directs the Literary Forum Press which in February 2020 began to publish *The Ledger*, a quarterly hard copy digest of the forum's activity. Currently Ali is working to organize and coordinate the six major online forums that treat Urdu literature, and in February 2020 at the annual Mother Languages Literary Festival in Islamabad, he gave a major address on social media and the internet as a medium for Urdu literature, outlining the structure of a multi-faceted site to serve writers and readers worldwide. Originally from Karachi, Pakistan, Ali is a practicing psychiatrist. He lives in Roanoke, Virginia.

Robert Schultz is an author and exhibiting artist. His previous books include three collections of poetry—most recently *Into the New World*—as well as a novel, a work of historical nonfiction, and a collaboration with photographer Binh Danh, *War Memoranda: Photography, Walt Whitman, and Memorials*. He has received a National Endowment for the Arts Literature Award, Cornell University's Corson Bishop Poetry Prize, and, from *Virginia Quarterly Review*, the Emily Clark Balch Prize for Poetry. Schultz's artwork is held by the U.S. Library of Congress, the University of Virginia special collections library, and by private collectors in the U.S. and abroad. He has spoken at Oxford University, the National Gallery of Art, and at colleges, universities, galleries, and museums. He has taught at Luther College, Cornell University, the University of Virginia, and served for 14 years as the John P. Fishwick Professor of English at Roanoke College. He now works full time as a writer and artist. He lives in Salem, Virginia.